1

Venice in the late Quattrocento

Before he signed the first of the canvases depicting the Stories from the Life of St Ursula, Vittore Carpaccio had only been mentioned in two documents: in the last will and testament drawn up on 21 September 1472 by his uncle Zuane Scarpazza (who had joined a monastery in Padua and was known as Brother Ilario), and in a receipt dated 8 August 1486 from which we learn that he paid the "Procuratie di Supra" in St Mark's for a building that his father Pietro, a leather merchant, was renting. This lack of documentation and the fact that we only have such a small number of paintings dating from before 1490, would suggest that

Vittore Carpaccio was born around 1465 and that he started training as a painter in the 1480s.

At around that time Venice was rapidly attaining the role of most triumphant and most wisely governed city in the West, to use the description given by Philippe de Commynes in his Memoirs; the diplomat Commynes had come to Venice in 1495 to prepare the way for Charles VIII's expedition. The Venetian Republic was still the major power in the Mediterranean and it continued in the wise policy of preserving as many as possible of its overseas possessions while at the same time improving its economic situation by enlarging its dominions on the mainland. Along the Grand Canal the number of flourishing foreign markets and warehouses increased, and the city gradually took on the appearance documented by Jacopo de' Barbari in his map dating from 1500. Stimulated by new cultural interests the young aristocrats no longer studied exclusively at the prestigious old University of Padua; they also followed the courses at the new School of Logic and Natural Philosophy, opened in Rialto at the beginning of the century, and at the Humanist School set up around the middle of the 15th century in the Chancery of St Mark's. In the last years of the century the printing and publishing industry developed, producing books on a wide range of topics from ancient and contemporary culture, primarily thanks to the activity of Aldo Manuzio who opened a printworks in Venice in 1489; among the texts published by Manuzio, the *Hypnerotomachia Poliphili*, printed in 1499, is one of the most important Venetian Humanist texts. And the development of scientific studies was also significant, including the 1494 publication of the text *Summa de Arithmetica, Geometria et Proportionalità*, by Luca Pacioli from Borgo San Sepolcro, a compatriot and admirer of Piero della Francesca, who came to Venice in the early 1470s to teach mathematics.

The flourishing cultural activity profoundly influenced all aspects of Venetian artistic development. After the last examples of the International Gothic style, the Ca' d'Oro and the Porta della Carta in the Doges' Palace, Pietro Lombardo, Codussi and Antonio Rizzo began to design their splendid marble constructions. And at the same time, all buildings, old and new, were further enriched with sculptures, precious objects, frescoes and paintings in the new Renaissance style. The last echoes of the International Gothic style had only just faded and the first, solitary representatives of the new Renaissance art, Jacopo Bellini and Antonio Vivarini, were still active; at this time the art scene in Venice was dominated by the followers of Donatello and other Tuscan artists, such as Paolo Uccello, Filippo Lippi and Andrea del Castagno, who all spent periods of time working in Padua and Venice. Not all the artists of the period produced innovative work. Bartolomeo Vivarini, following the example of Mantegna, was interested in the sculptural quality of his images; Gentile Bellini painted lengthy celebratory tales of sacred and profane stories, in a style that shows a certain nostalgia for the art of the Middle Ages. Giovanni Bellini offered the first great, poetic interpretation of painting in Venice: through his perfectly orchestrated harmony of space, light

2

2. *St Martin and the Beggar*
112 x 72 cm
Zadar, Cathedral

3. *The Pilgrims' Arrival in Cologne, detail*
Venice, Accademia

and colour he gives us a new vision of man and the world, freed from the transcendental ideas of the Middle Ages, a vision elaborated in Tuscany in the early part of the 15th century thanks to the laws of linear perspective. Alongside Giovanni Bellini, we find Alvise Vivarini, Bartolomeo Montagna, Benedetto Diana, Giambattista Cima, all interested primarily in architectural compositions, in accurate drawing, in the three-dimensional quality of forms moulded by light, in enamel-like colours, following the example of the works painted by Antonello da Messina in Venice in 1475-76.

In this lively and varied artistic climate, open also to the influences of Flemish painting and Northern European prints and etchings that

Francesco Valcanover

CARPACCIO

SCALA/RIVERSIDE

CONTENTS

To Maria Giovanna
July 4, 1988

© Copyright 1989 by SCALA, Istituto Fotografico
Editoriale, S.p.A., Antella (Firenze)
Editing: Karin Stephan
Translation: Lisa Pelletti
Layout: Fried Rosenstock
Photographs: SCALA (M. Falsini and M. Sarri) except:
no. 2 (Revija, Belgrade); no. 29 (Paul Getty Museum,
Malibu); no. 35 (Blauel-Gnamm Artothek, Munich); nos.
36, 60 and 61 (National Gallery of Art, Washington);
no. 37 (Metropolitan Museum of Art, New York); no.
57 (Gulbenkian Foundation, Lisbon); nos. 62 and 71
(Staatsgalerie, Stuttgart); no. 65 (Thyssen Collection,
Lugano); nos. 66, 67, 76 and 77 (Gemäldegalerie
Dahlem, Berlin)
Produced by SCALA
Printed in Italy by Lito Terrazzi, Cascine del Riccio
Florence 1989

1. The Blessing Redeemer between Four Apostles
70 x 68 cm
Florence, property of the Contini Bonacossi heirs

spread quite rapidly at that period, Vittore Carpaccio received his first artistic training. The *Blessing Redeemer between Four Apostles*, in the Contini-Bonacossi Collection in Florence, is signed on the marble parapet VETOR SCARPAZO; already in this painting we can see quite clearly the influence that Antonello da Messina and his follower Alvise Vivarini had on the young painter. Arranged in a semi-circle, the Apostles stand out against the dark background in a rather implausible raised perspective foreshortening around the figure of Christ, who is portrayed frontally, while his hands, one imparting the blessing and the other holding the orb, appear almost to be testing the depth of the surrounding space, beyond the parapet; it is almost as though Carpaccio was practising the techniques observed in the work of Antonello. Equally evident is the influence of Northern European art, especially Flemish, in the precise observation of the features of the characters and the attention to details. Carpaccio was not as interested as Giovanni Bellini in the communication of mood; in his work colour is subordinated to modelling, a very meticulous graphic drawing of the faces and the rumpled folds of the cloth made sharper and brighter by the lighting, and achieving results similar to the art of Bartolomeo Montagna. Despite attributions to Carpaccio, the *Madonna and Child with Saints* in the Civic Museum in Vicenza is without doubt the work of Montagna.

The attempt to give his forms a sculptural quality and to place them inside a constructed space modelled on Antonello's art, with all the naturalness of Giovanni Bellini's use of colour, is evident again in the *Dead Christ*, in the Contini-Bonacossi Collection in Florence. Here, the figures of the Virgin, of Joseph of Arimathaea and John the Baptist are crowded round the Saviour's body and barely fit inside the frame.

3

And in the polyptych in the Cathedral of St Anastasia in Zadar, Yugoslavia, where the central panels show *St Jerome and the Donor*, and *St Martin and the Beggar*, large figures placed against a landscape of rocky hills, in a spatial and perspective construction as paradoxical as a composition by Gentile Bellini.

The Stories from the Life of St Ursula and contemporary works

The young Carpaccio's clumsy perspective construction, so noticeable in the *Blessing Redeemer between Four Apostles* and in the Zadar Polyptych, also characterizes the first painting that we can date with certainty, the *Pilgrims' Arrival in Cologne*, one of the episodes from the St Ursula cycle. The Confraternity of St Ursula, founded on 15 July 1300, had its headquarters in a small building next to the southern apse of the Dominican church of Santi Giovanni e Paolo. On 16 November 1488 the Confraternity decided to commission a series of large canvases recounting the story of St Ursula. The legend of this northern saint was extremely popular in the Middle Ages and had been the subject of several pictorial cycles; among the ones that Carpaccio must have studied before beginning his own, undoubtedly one of the most important would have been the

4

frescoes that Tommaso da Modena painted between 1355 and 1358 in the chapel of St Ursula in the church of Santa Margherita in Treviso (now in the Civic Museum). And he would also have read Jacobus de Voragine's *Legenda Aurea*, probably in Nicolò Malerbi's Italian translation, printed by Jenson in Venice in 1475. The aspects of this tragic story of love and death that particularly strike Carpaccio are the more festive and celebratory elements; the arrival of the ambas-

4, 5. The Pilgrims' Arrival in Cologne
280 x 255 cm
Venice, Accademia

6. Martyrdom of the Pilgrims and the Funeral of St Ursula
271 x 561 cm
Venice, Accademia

5

6

7

7. *Apotheosis of St Ursula, detail*
Venice, Accademia

8. *Apotheosis of St Ursula*
481 x 336 cm
Venice, Accademia

sadors of the pagan King of England at the Court of the Christian King of Brittany, to ask for the hand of his daughter Ursula for the son of their Lord; the conditions Ursula sets out before accepting the marriage proposal; the farewells and Ursula's pilgrimage; the dream in which Ursula is forewarned of her martyrdom; her encounter with Pope Cyriacus in Rome; her arrival in Cologne, occupied by the Huns; the slaughter of the pilgrims and Ursula's funeral; and lastly, the altarpiece with St Ursula in glory above the host of martyrs.

In painting the nine canvases, today in the Accademia in Venice, Carpaccio was not able to follow the chronological order of the story. In order to make room for the canvases two altars and two sarcophagi of deceased members of the Confraternity (including the tomb of the Loredan family, patrons of the School) had to be removed;

and Carpaccio was forced to paint the scenes in the order that the wallspace was made available to him. He began working in 1490 and did not complete the cycle until shortly after 1495, the year he painted the *Meeting of the Betrothed* 12 *Couple and the Departure of the Pilgrims*. In fact, a recent interpretation of the *De origine situ et magistratibus urbis Venetae*, which Sanudo dedicated to Doge Agostino Barbarigo in 1493, suggests that in that year a large portion of the cycle was already finished: "A San Zuane Pollo... la capella de Sant'Orsola, le historie et figure che è atorno, bellissime..."

The evolution of Carpaccio's visual language is astonishing: in just over five years his art has developed to such poetic heights that he challenges the supremacy of Giovanni Bellini, until then the unrivalled master of the Venetian art scene.

In the scene of the *Pilgrims' Arrival in Cologne* 4 some details of the event are relegated to marginal positions. While in the distance some of the vessels of the retinue are still out at sea, to the left the flagship has already docked; Ursula and Pope 5 Cyriacus lean out to ask information from a boatman. To the right, in the foreground, four armed envoys have just finished reading out the message warning the Hun princes of the arrival of the Christian pilgrims. Carpaccio does not really demonstrate great self-assuredness in the composition of the scene or in the way the individual events are related to one another. But we can already begin to make out the characteristic features of his visual language: the slow, almost magically suspended rhythm of the narration, fixed in its most salient moment; the attention to the lighting of even the smallest details; the extraordinary brightness of the colours. The event is portrayed in a fresh and lively scene of movement. At the top, the vessel's pennant and the mast are cut off abruptly, while to the left there is the suggestion of a vast expanse of water and to the right the urban density of Cologne. The setting is reminiscent of a misty autumn morning in Venice. In the greyish light the ships glide slowly over the still water, reaching the harbour just outside the city walls depicted in perspective towards a vanishing point on the horizon: this whole part of the scene looks very much like the older sections of the Arsenal in Venice.

When looking at this painting of the *Pilgrims' Arrival in Cologne*, one cannot help but think of the young Carpaccio's favourite parts of Venice: the Doges' Palace, the Scuola di San Girolamo, the Chapter Halls of the Scuola Grande di San Marco and of the Scuola di San Giovanni Evangelista, containing permanent exhibitions of paint-

8

9

ings of Venetian history and ceremonies. And Vittore Carpaccio must have been especially fascinated by the beauty of the colours and the fairytale nature of the narrative paintings of Gentile da Fabriano and Pisanello, which he saw also in the more modern re-elaborations, full of Humanist overtones, in the canvases and drawings of Jacopo Bellini. And he must also have noticed how those rather timid space and perspective constructions had not really developed much in the vast, stage-like compositions by Gentile Bellini, and were actually impoverished and reduced to the level of an inanimate chronicle in the work of his mediocre followers, Lazzaro Bastiani and Giovanni Mansueti. And although he must indeed have been fascinated by the "modern" painting of Giovanni Bellini, he felt that his vocation was to follow the example of Alvise Vivarini

9. The Pilgrims Meet the Pope
281 x 307 cm
Venice, Accademia

10. The Pilgrims Meet the Pope,
detail of St Ursula and Pope Cyriacus
Venice, Accademia

11. Tommaso da Modena
St Ursula Meets the Pope
Treviso, Civic Museum

and Bartolomeo Montagna, disciples and imitators of Antonello da Messina.

The *Apotheosis of St Ursula and her Followers,* 8 signed and dated 1491 on the cartouche below the circle of angels' heads around the palm-trunk, is also one of the earlier canvases of the cycle.

10

11

The theory, supported by some scholars, that this altarpiece actually dates from 1510 when Carpaccio supposedly repainted it since the original version had been badly damaged, has been disproved by a recent X-ray of the whole painting (which has, incidentally, revealed that the three splendid male portraits to the left are later additions). But the theory can also be disproved by a stylistic analysis: compare it, for instance, to the *Presentation in the Temple*, which dates from around 1510, also in the Accademia. The complexity of the perspective foreshortening of the marble aedicula, of the furled banners, of the figure of Ursula surrounded by angels and with God the Father looking down at her, is far too self-conscious and still too close to the style of Mantegna to be the work of the established artist active around 1510. Both the central episode of the composition and the heads of the virgin martyrs crowded in the lower part of the painting show quite clearly that this altarpiece dates from

7

63

13

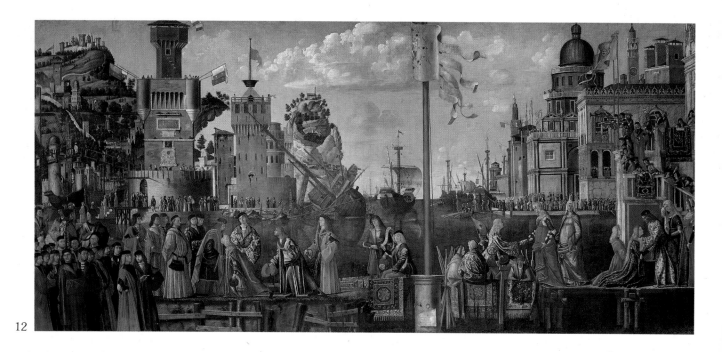

12

12. Meeting of the Betrothed Couple and the Departure of the Pilgrims
280 x 611 cm
Venice, Accademia

the same stylistic period as the painting depicting the *Pilgrims' Arrival in Cologne*. And even the artist's reluctance to reconcile the devotional and iconographical aspect of the work to the narrative and dramatic elements, which he was more interested in, suggest an early dating. The most poetic element of this painting are certainly the two Venetian landscape details, with their lively and fresh colours, and the loving precision with which he describes the hills, the urban fabric, the countryside, the events of daily life.

This same colour tone and mood, but used in a much more self-assured perspective composition, appears again in the *Meeting between Pope Cyriacus and the Pilgrims*. Scholars do not agree on the dating of this canvas and suggestions go from 1491, the same year as the *Apotheosis of St Ursula*, to 1493, the year of the *Martyrdom of the Pilgrims and the Funeral of St Ursula*. Even the question of the identification of the character in red standing next to Pope Cyriacus as Ermolao Barbaro, an eminent Humanist and the Venetian ambassador to the Vatican who died in 1493 after having fallen out of grace in Venice, is used in different ways by the advocates of the various chronological theories. The style of the canvas would appear to suggest a more mature period than the *Pilgrims' Arrival in Cologne* canvas, which dates from 1490.

The scene of the meeting takes place in the bright afternoon light: to the left, the retinue of virgins is shown approaching along the path, while the English Prince and Ursula, in the centre, kneel in front of Pope Cyriacus; and to the right the procession of bishops, prelates and dignitaries unfolds in the bright, sunlit meadow outside the

walls of Rome. Each figure projects its own shadow to emphasize the hour of the day in which the historic meeting is taking place; like a brilliant colour prism it revolves slowly in an atmosphere of absolute enchantment. The calculated stage-like arrangement of the characters is echoed in the setting of the eight standards, the white mitres, the regular geometric shapes of the huge construction of Castel Sant'Angelo. Not even the tiniest of details is lost on this enormous stage: the lavish ornamentation of the damask copes, or the group of clarion players standing out against the sky on the castle's bastions, or the ivy clinging to the walls.

The speed at which Carpaccio's ideas develop is noticeable in the *Martyrdom of the Pilgrims and the Funeral of St Ursula*, signed and dated 1493 on the scroll at the foot ot the column bearing two coats-of-arms, the emblem of the Loredan family and another one, probably belonging to the Caotorta family. The composition of the scene is quite complex, for Carpaccio wanted to include two separate episodes from the legend of St Ursula in the same painting, one being the violent scene of the slaughter of the pilgrims and the other the sad and mournful description of the saint's funeral: he succeeds thanks to his masterly spatial division of the composition. The focus of the painting is the knight about to draw his sword out of its scabbard; notice how similar he is to cer-

14

13. *Meeting of the Betrothed Couple and the
Departure of the Pilgrims, detail
Venice, Accademia*

14

*14-16. Meeting of the Betrothed Couple and the
Departure of the Pilgrims, details
Venice, Accademia*

tain figures by Perugino. Behind him, the moorish
bugler on horseback rallies the troops and the
white and red standard gives depth to the background landscape, mellowed by the green
meadow and the pinkish buildings depicted in the
peaceful light of the Venetian pre-Alps. Right in
the foreground, on the edge of the field in which
the knights look almost as though they were taking part in a mediaeval tournament, a fair-haired
archer draws the bow he holds in his gloved hand
— he is like a sophisticated arabesque in his elegant pose and splendid costume. Motionless, Ursula awaits the mortal arrow, standing against a
background of trees, arranged like the wings of a
stage, that seem to prolong the scene of the
slaughter all the way to infinity. But, just like the
fresco of this same episode painted by Tommaso
da Modena more than a century earlier, every
gesture, even the most violent, is part of a deliber-
ate rhythm and a strict geometric pattern com-
posed of the interplay of weapons of all sorts:
swords, daggers, misericords, bludgeons, pikes,
spears and halberds, each carefully described
down to the tiniest details.

The calculated violence of the scene of the

slaughter is separated from the solemnly dignified scene of Ursula's funeral by a column on a pedestal of a very complex shape and colour scheme. This second event is indissolubly linked to the first since they are both set in the unmistakable atmosphere of the Venetian mainland landscape. The funeral procession solemnly parades out of the town at the foot of the wooded hill, and marches towards the mausoleum; all that we can see of the mausoleum is one marble corner, in the shadow, with a carved inscription reading URSULA. Against the vibrant luminosity of the blue sky, the landscape, the human beings and the architectural constructions appear almost like a colourful inlay. All the characters, portraits of contemporaries, take part in this splendid interplay of forms, with their statuary solidity and their sense of physical movement; notice particularly the woman kneeling to the right, presumably a deceased member of the Caotorta family since she is portrayed set apart from the rest of the procession.

As time passed, Carpaccio gradually became more and more involved in an abstract and conceptual kind of art, but one that was linked to the portrayal of the truth, with wide-ranging expanses arranged along perspective lines constructed around deep and broad spaces, with a use of the most splendid local colour tonalities and exploration of details that was totally naturalistic.

12 The *Meeting of the Betrothed Couple and the Departure of the Pilgrims*, signed and dated 1495, is the largest painting in the cycle and actually contains six different episodes of the legend.
13 To the left Ereus takes leave of his father; to the right of the pennant, on top of which the banner is shown blowing in the wind, we see the
15 betrothed couple at their first meeting, as they take their leave from Ursula's parents, as they board the twelve-oared sloop and then the ship; to the left we see the ship again, its sail billowing in the wind, and the inscription MALO is rather like a foreboding of the tragic fate that lies ahead for the pilgrims. In the most natural way all the various moments of the story follow on each other without interruption, within the carefully constructed composition. Within this unitary space, the free and varied vibration of the lighting makes even the smallest details totally plausible, created as they are by brushstrokes of unfailing precision. This kaleidoscopic pageant also con-
13 tains very realistic elements, such as the two towers of the Knights of Rhodes and St Mark of Candia, probably modelled on woodcuts by Reeuwich illustrating the *Peregrinatio in Terram Sanctam* by Breydenbach that was printed in Mainz in

17

17. *St Ursula's Dream*
Florence, Uffizi Gallery Drawings Collection

1486; Carpaccio has placed these two towers on the steep slopes of the hill protected by walls, towers and castles. While the English city is surrounded by an impregnable set of walls and towers, on the other side of the canvas the city in Brittany stretches out totally defenceless, built along the water's edge, full of buildings with elegant marble facades. These are clearly reproductions of the palaces that Codussi and the Lombardo brothers were building in Venice towards the end of the 15th century and which were rapidly changing the appearance of the city. The characters in the foreground are clustered together in groups to the left, on the quarter deck and on the pier stretching out from the harbour over the greenish water; they are all wearing clothes in keeping with the fashions of the time, each one according to his age and social standing. Notice the splendid young man to the left of the pennant, with the 14 coat-of-arms of the Fratelli Zardinieri, one of the Compagnie della Calza, embroidered on his sleeve. As is the case during traditional and religious celebrations that still take place in Venice today, the streets, bridges, alleyways and steps are crowded with onlookers and many more are shown looking out of the windows; in the background of the painting we can see the caulkers working on a huge ship, dry docked and lying on its side. And the Breton and English cities in the distance are also hives of activity. In the clear air one can almost hear the trumpets and the drums beating at the foot of the tower and on the bastions, the screeching of the halyards against the

18

18. St Ursula's Dream
274 x 267 cm
Venice, Accademia

blocks stretching the sails billowing in the wind and even the scratching of the goosequill on the parchment on which the diligent scribe in the upper righthand corner is recording the highpoints of the event and the names of the most important protagonists.

Carpaccio's masterful ability at grasping each detail while still preserving the unity of the scene and its symbolic value reaches its peak in this cycle in the painting of the *Dream*. In the preparatory drawings, now in the Drawings Collection in the Uffizi in Florence, there is an intensely lyrical feeling of space, which in the painting becomes even more magical and enchanted. The elements of reality are arranged in perfect perspective constructions, creating scenes that will remain part of our memory for the rest of time: he is capable of describing a late Quattrocento Venetian bedroom with an objectivity that reminds one of Vermeer. Below a canopy supported by tall thin rods, the sleeping Ursula is visited in her dreams by the an-

16
18 17

20

*19, 20. Arrival of the English Ambassadors, details
Venice, Accademia*

gel (notice the sharp shadow he casts on the ground) who tells her of her imminent martyrdom. The light shines brightly behind the angel and penetrates into the room from the roundels below the beams, from the windows and from the half-open door leading into the next room; but it does not succeed in dispelling all the shadows in the bedroom. In this chiaroscuro atmosphere, every detail is rendered with subdued light and soft shadows: the little slippers, the gold crown and the little dog at the foot of the bed; the little table with the hourglass on it and the book, still open at the page where Ursula stopped reading; the pots on the window ledge with carnations and myrtle growing in them, plants that symbolize earthly and heavenly love; the holy image lit by the smoking candle that we can see through the elaborately carved frame and the equally richly carved chair below it; the antique gilded bronze statuettes of Hercules and Venus above the door-

frames; the cupboard with its doors ajar so that we can see its contents.

The three paintings of the Ambassadors are evidence of the extent to which Carpaccio's feeling for colour had developed; in them the artist displays his extraordinary ability at directing or staging pageants and religious celebrations of the kind that must have been fairly frequent at the time. In the painting of the *English Ambassadors' Arrival at the Court of the King of Brittany*, the first episode of the cycle of Stories from the Life of St Ursula, the splendid achitectural setting, with the open loggia against the background of a view of Venice and the intimate space of the private room, divides the scene into two sections: the ambassadors deliver their message on one side and Ursula discusses the matter with her father on the other. The entire composition is arranged with absolute self-confidence and accuracy. In the diplomatic ceremony the afternoon light streams in from the left and illuminates the foreground, with patches of bright colours and sharp shadows. Below the wide portico that stretches out to the left with a row of arcades vanishing into the dis-

21

21

tance, alternating with areas of shadow, the elegant young members of the Compagnia della Calza are portrayed in poses of the most self-assured nonchalance, and showing indifference for what is happening nearby. To the right of the elaborate candelabrum, with marble and bright metal decorations, a sophisticated ornamentation that is reminiscent of the work of Ferrarese artists, the English ambassadors are received by King Maurus; they are portrayed in attitudes of deference and respect, in keeping with the rigid protocol governing public audiences granted by the Vene-

21, 22. Arrival of the English Ambassadors, details
Venice, Accademia

23. Arrival of the English Ambassadors
275 x 589 cm
Venice, Accademia

tian Republican institutions at the time. The King 21 sits, like the Doge, amidst his counsellors on a judgment seat against a wall covered in precious ornamented leather hangings, placed at an angle to the light and opening out onto a view of the city

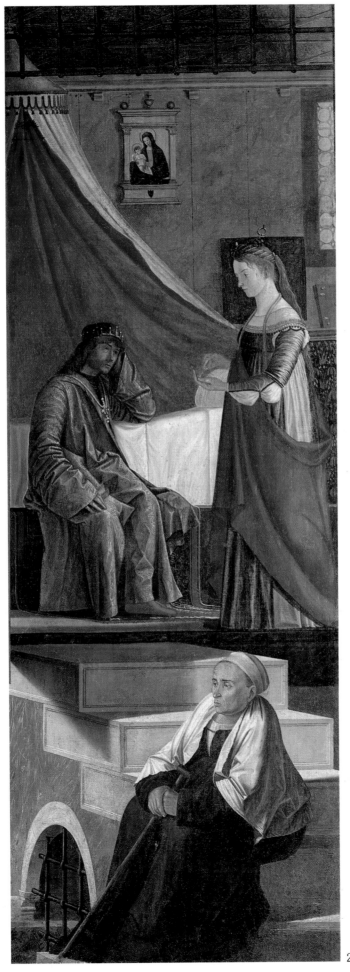

23

24

24, 25. The Ambassadors Depart
280 x 253 cm
Venice, Accademia

26

dominated by a round domed temple-like construction, reminiscent of Perugino and almost anticipating Baldassarre Longhena's Santa Maria della Salute. Just as the colours of the architecture are reflected in the water, so the shadows of the small figures fall like dark stripes on the red brick and white marble expanse of the square bathed in warm sunlight. Although the buildings and the landscape are quite definitely Venetian in character, it is not possible to identify them as specific constructions. And even the many identifications of the people in the painting with contemporaries of Carpaccio's are all purely hypothetical. The most fascinating theory is the identification of the man in the red cloak to the left, outside the main scene of the event, looking towards the spectator: he is traditionally supposed to be either Pietro Loredan, one of the patrons who commissioned the decoration of the Scuola, or a self-portrait. He stands in front of the iron banister enclosing the scene and appears almost to be drawing our attention towards the ambassadors and their message; like the young boy with the long feather on his cap who also looks out towards the spectator, a detail that was only recently (1983) rediscovered thanks to an excellent cleaning job. The nurse sitting at the far right in an attitude of resignation, on the other hand, introduces us to the conversation between Maurus and his daughter, which does not take place in an elegant and formal hall like the audience of the ambassador, but in the domestic intimacy of Ursula's bedroom.

26, 27. The Ambassadors Return to the English Court
297 x 527 cm
Venice, Accademia

The King has abandoned all the official royal formalities imposed by protocol and simply listens to the conditions set out by his daughter. She will marry Ereus if she is granted a retinue of ten beautiful virgins; she and each of the ten shall further be assigned a thousand virgins each; and the young man who has asked for her hand shall be baptized and instructed in the faith for a period of three years. The two figures, father and daughter, are set against the canopy of the bed and the wall decorated with a devotional icon in an inversion of patches of colour that is almost an anticipation of the art of Paolo Veronese. And the harmony of colours with which Carpaccio depicts the old governess is equally masterful: she sits at the foot of the stairway leading to Ursula's bedroom and stares out into space, as though she knew what a tragic ending this royal wedding contract would lead to. Years later Titian was obviously so struck by this figure of the governess that he included a modern version of her in the *Presentation of the Virgin* that he painted between 1536 and 1538 for the Scuola Grande di Santa Maria della Carità.

In the scene of the *Ambassadors Depart* Carpaccio takes us back to the formalities of an offi-

cial ceremony. The interior of the diplomatic Chancery is constructed round the interplay of various perspective foreshortenings, like the huge corridor with the stairway above the grandiose arch through which we can see the sky. As far as the eye can see the sharp outdoor light emphasizes every detail, each depicted with absolute perfection and purity of form: the marble ornamentations, with the play of light and shadow in the colourful geometric patterns; the extraordinary candelabrum; the pure white sculpture that stands out against the gold niche, its surface so smooth that it looks like a work by Antonio Rizzo; the characters arranged in poses and attitudes suited to their role and function. The regal dignity of Maurus and his counsellors, some portrayed in splendid profile poses, is counterbalanced by the deferential homage being paid by the ambassadors, a contrast that is repeated in the figures of 25 the haughty secretary and the humble scribe. Next to the bored-looking child in the red tunic, who observes his fellow in brown, shown reading, a gentleman introduces us to the ceremony with his left hand. The description of the crowd gathered along the steps and leaning against the balustrades of the building in the background is equally accurate. Everything is portrayed with great attention to detail, in the most perfect interaction of space, forms, light and colours, an anti-41 cipation of the *Vision of St Augustine*, the masterpiece of the cycle that Carpaccio painted in the early years of the 16th century for the Scuola di San Giorgio degli Schiavoni.

26 The canvas showing the *Return of the Ambassadors to the English Court* also contains views of Venice and scenes from the everyday reality of the city in the late 15th century. See, for example, at the far left of the painting, next to the marble base that supports the pennant from which the standard is shown flapping in the sea breeze, the seated "scalco" or steward with his club and his gold chain, and the boy playing the rebec, both of them protagonists of the Venetian Republic's ceremonial protocol for receiving newly arrived foreign delegations. The view of the city is domi-27 nated by the splendid Renaissance palace, almost a symbol of Vittore Carpaccio's architectural painting. The description of the interiors is suggested by the volumetric structure of the building, whose wide arch depicted in deep shadow recalls the buildings painted about twenty years earlier by Antonello da Messina in his *St Sebastian* for the church of San Giuliano in Venice (the painting is now in the Gemäldegalerie in Dresden). The facades consist of luminous surfaces, enclosed by frames of projecting cornices and strips of coloured marble, decorated with marble bas-reliefs of classical subjects and with an extremely elegant row of windows opening onto a wide balcony. The diagonal perspective lines of this majestic construction, whose perfect architectural forms are reminiscent of the buildings that Codussi was designing at around that time, provide the basic structure on which all the elements of the composition are arranged: the bridge and the banks full of spectators, each carefully portrayed in costumes that denote social standing and origin; the pinkish brick paving, surrounded by the green grass of the "campo"; the octagonal royal pavilion; the two mediaeval towers in the background, protecting the canal. The enchanted magic of the different planes, set out in the perfect construction of this ideal geometrical form, is paralleled in the rich density of the colours; in the pale lighting of this late spring morning the colours take on entirely new tonalities, especially in the shining silk costumes and in the imaginative headdresses. And, as always, Carpaccio grasps every last detail, like the swift trireme that has just docked at the pier next to a "cocca," the typical Venetian freight vessel, or the casements of the balcony crowded with people, silvery cylinders of glass, some of which are broken.

In the last paintings of the St Ursula cycle, Carpaccio reaches the peak of his visual poetry. Such a rapid artistic evolution was the result of a series of influences, and actually we can say that Carpaccio was by this stage one of the most cultured artists of his day. In his work we can distinguish Antonello da Messina's carefully planned synthesis of light and colour and the optical precision of Flemish painters; the colour tonalities of the lyrical world of Giovanni Bellini and the rational subtlety of the sacred and profane narration that flourished in Ferrara as a result of the meeting between the Paduan Andrea Mantegna, the Tuscan Piero della Francesca and the Flemish artist Rogier van der Weyden; the measured and luminous elegance of the architecture of Pietro Lombardo and Codussi; and Perugino's suspension of emotion. These fundamental components of the style of Vittore Carpaccio, which scholars have written about at length, evolved into his very personal visual language over a brief period, hardly more than five years, from the time he began work on the St Ursula cycle to when he completed it. Ever

28. Man with a Red Cap
35 x 23 cm
Venice, Correr Museum

since the first canvases, which reflect both his youthful enthusiasm and his inexperience, his way of depicting reality and the daily life of the period, free from hierarchical constraints, is neither an objective chronicle nor the inconclusive analysis typical of genre painting. Very early on his compositions become self-confident constructions containing wide panoramic views in perspective foreshortening and with great depth of field. Every detail, even the most insignificant, is carefully executed from a formal point of view. Free from emotional drama, even in the most violent episodes, the protagonists of this chivalric tale are depicted in a symbolic suspension made up of elementary physical gestures and spiritual expression, as though they were on the stage of an imaginary theatre. In this world, which is quite different from the irregularity and corruption of the real world, even the remotest and most negligible detail becomes one of importance and has been studied and painted as an autonomous and vital element, with all the care of a modern designer. In the elaboration of such a figurative precision the main elements are colour and light; and as the years go by Carpaccio will blend them in a totally innovative way. The colour tonalities he uses do not share the natural, atmospheric quality of Giovanni Bellini's, nor do they become crystallized into the translucid colour patches of the followers of Antonello or the Flemish artists; they preserve the concreteness of pictorial matter, reflecting and vibrating in values and tones that are purely local.

Against the green meadows or the blue skies streaked with thin clouds, against the pink brick buildings that are as brilliant as any marble facing, in the foreground we find resplendent costumes, with carefully calculated colour harmonies, while rapid brushstrokes construct with perfect accuracy and infallible speed the semblances of reality. The limpid quality of the light is an indispensable element in such a perfect colour composition. The light softly skims over the brick surfaces, it beats down on the polychrome pavings, on the veined marble, on the bare dirt ground of the squares; it rests on the green masses of the trees and creates pearly reflections on the fleshtones and on the costumes; it embraces the distant sun-drenched views of water and hillsides; it falls sharply into the interiors, here intense and blinding, there soft and dense, but always capable of creating lively reflections in a continuous subtle game with the shadows. In this staged display, made more fascinating by colour and light, in a preordained but totally natural order, the artist places the actors and spectators of his chivalric tale, each observed with total detachment, as though they were the contemporary characters of distant events. And Carpaccio does not hesitate to give us precise portrayals of individuals and of states of mind. Many of the characters are in fact probably members of the Confraternity of the Scuola and other notable Venetians of the period, including the Loredan family, patrons of the Scuola and quite likely the artist's first clients. These presences, in this sacred story turned into secular pageantry, emanate an intense memory of late 15th-century Venice. And indeed the calm expanses of water streaked with colourful reflections could only be Venetian; or the galleys with their billowing sails, ready to set off for the open seas; the gondolas and the barges heading for the safe harbours on the islands; the palaces with their precious marble decorations and the pink brick buildings, all topped by typical Venetian roof terraces and round chimneytops; the alleys and walkways along the canals, the bridges, the piers, the raised steps, the balconies crowded with people; the costumes and every little detail of the Venetian daily life of the period. And Carpaccio reproduces with the same lively accuracy the realities of the Venetian mainland, the gentle hills at the foot of the mountains, the walled cities, the countryside showing evidence of the industrious presence of man.

Although the chronology of Vittore Carpaccio's work is fairly complex and cannot easily be correlated or compared to the network of influences and trends developed by the other artists active at the time, there is a group of paintings that can undoubtedly be dated at the early 1490s since they are so close stylistically to the Stories from the Life of St Ursula. Among them, the *Man with the Red Cap* in the Correr Museum in Venice, which has incorrectly been attributed in the past to Lotto and to Bartolomeo Montagna. Standing out with almost sculptural relief from the landscape background, this figure shares the proud expression of the portraits Carpaccio painted of his contemporaries even in the earliest of the St Ursula cycle canvases. The *Portrait of a Lady* in the Denver Art Museum in Colorado, as we can see also from the preparatory drawing in the Christ Church Library Collection in Oxford, exhibits this same self-confidence. And even the hunting scene now in the Paul Getty Museum in Malibu, California, an extraordinary image set in the enchanted

29. Hunting on the Lagoon
76 x 65 cm
Malibu (California), Paul Getty Museum

30

silence of the lagoon in a bird's eye view of incredible realism, appears to have been painted only shortly before the scene in the lefthand section of the *Arrival of the Ambassadors*, with the gondola gliding on the still waters towards a safe mooring place on the nearby island.

It was quite probably thanks to the fame Carpaccio had won for himself with the Stories from the Life of St Ursula that he was called upon by the Confraternity of the Scuola Grande di San Giovanni Evangelista to paint one of the canvases for the Great Hall of their headquarters showing the *Miracles of the Holy Cross*, the story of the miracles performed by the fragment of wood from the Cross on which Jesus was crucified; this fragment had been donated to the brotherhood in 1369 by Philip de Mezieres, Chancellor of the Kingdom of Cyprus and Jerusalem, and had

soon become an object of great veneration and the symbol of the Scuola, one of the most important and wealthy Venetian confraternities. In this new task Vittore Carpaccio worked together with Pietro Perugino and the most respected Venetian painters of the period, including Gentile Bellini, Giovanni Mansueti, Lazzaro Bastiani and Benedetto Diana. The canvas painted by Perugino has been lost, but the eight surviving paintings, executed between 1496 and 1501, contain depictions of some of the most famous parts of Venice. Since they are all in the Accademia now it is easy to compare them: we notice immediately the

32

32. *Miracle of the Relic of the Holy Cross, detail*
Venice, Accademia

33. *Gentile Bellini*
Procession in St Mark's
Venice, Accademia

34. *Christ and Four Angels*
162 x 163 cm
Udine, Civic Museum

basic difference between the archaic choice of images, sometimes portrayed purely as a sort of inventory, offered by the older artists and the new, lively depictions of the city painted by Carpaccio. His painting dates from 1496 or later and illustrates the episode of the healing of a possessed man: the Patriarch of Grado, Francesco Querini, cured the man thanks to the fragment of the Cross. The scene takes place in the Patriarch's palace at San Silvestro on the Grand Canal near

30

33

35

Almost as in a snapshot, the artist shows us the private gondolas and those used to ferry people 32 across the canal and how they leave their trail in the slate-coloured water of the Grand Canal; the notables and the elegant members of the Compagnia della Calza are gathered in conversation under the loggia of the Patriarch of Grado's palace; the procession marches slowly over the bridge, and it is easy to distinguish the visiting Oriental dignitaries among the crowd. Everywhere people are busy in their daily activities: the women beat their rugs and squeeze the water out of their washing; the cooper is rinsing out his new 31 wine barrel; the masons are putting new tiles on the roof. Carpaccio's exploration of reality is based on his accurate pictorial rendering, obtained thanks to a naturalistic use of lighting and colour tonalities. Against the dark, slate-coloured water of the Grand Canal, against the pinkish blue of the sky streaked with thin clouds, the images make up a colourful inlay, of an optical accuracy that would not be matched in Venice again till Canaletto's vedutas.

To go from Carpaccio's *Miracle of the Relic of the Holy Cross at Rialto* to the other scene of a miracle, this time taking place in St Mark's 33 Square, that Gentile Bellini painted in 1496 is like changing universe. While in Gentile's canvas iconographical fidelity is frozen in a huge pageantry transposed into a poetically archaic composition of forms and colours, which feels almost as though it has had the air removed from it, in Carpaccio's painting the reproduction of the details of city life takes shape in rational and realistic images which evoke the wide open space with incomparable naturalism.

In the last five years of the 15th century, while he was completing the St Ursula cycle and was working on the large canvas for the Scuola di San Giovanni Evangelista, Vittore Carpaccio painted a few other smaller-scale sacred subjects; in them he appears to be influenced, as never before, by the human gentleness of Giovanni Bellini's ideal dreams. The first is probably the *Christ and Four 34 Angels* that he painted in 1496 for the church of San Pietro Martire in Udine and which is today in the Civic Museum in that same city. Against the red damask curtain the ivory-coloured emaciated body of Christ stands out in the light; he is shown in a mood of subtle melancholy, devoid of

Rialto bridge. The actual miracle is set in the spacious loggia in the top lefthand corner, so that the view of this part of the city can take up as much space as possible. Set along a diagonal line, with the Albergo dello Storione (the Sturgeon Inn, the sign is clearly legible) at the centre, the view goes all the way to the end of the Riva del Vin at the Rialto bridge. The bridge is depicted as it appeared before its collapse in August 1524. Built entirely in wood, it housed two rows of shops, just like today's stone bridge built in 1591; in the middle it could open up to allow large freight ships to sail past and deliver their wares to the numerous storehouses along the banks of the Grand Canal. On the other side of the wooden construction of the bridge, on the left we can make out a loggia which was used as a meeting place by all the merchants attending the Rialto market, one of the largest in the whole of the Western world. To the right, amidst the numerous constructions, one can easily identify the 15th-century Fondaco dei Tedeschi (which burnt down in January 1505 and was rebuilt by 1508), the bell-tower of San Giovanni Crisostomo, the portico built along the waterfront of Ca' da Mosto, one of the very few Venetian Byzantine constructions that has survived, and the bell-tower of the church of Santi Apostoli, before it was rebuilt in 1672. This extremely accurate description of the buildings is paralleled in the realistic portrayal of the daily life.

36. Flight into Egypt
73 x 111 cm
Washington, National Gallery of Art

pietism, as are the four angels bearing the instruments of the Passion, towards which the two landscapes bathed in the silvery light of dawn converge diagonally.

This is also the period when Carpaccio painted the polyptych in the parish church of Grumello (Bergamo). The two panels showing *St James* and *St Jerome in Penance*, in the relationship between the human bodies and the landscape, are also very similar to two paintings of the same subjects done by Giovanni Bellini, now in the Contini-Bonacossi Collection in Florence and in the National Gallery in London. Also modelled on paintings by Bellini are the *Madonna and Child with the Young St John the Baptist* in the Städelsches Kunstinstitut in Frankfurt and the *Madonna and Child with Saints Cecilia and Ursula*, which formerly belonged to the Morosini family and is now in an English private collection; the two allegorical figures of *Prudence* and *Temperance*, now in the Atlanta Art Association Galleries, are also similar in mood and composition. Two of Bellini's masterpieces dating from the 1480s, the *Dead Christ Supported by Angels* in

the Pinacoteca Civica in Rimini and the other one now in the National Gallery in London, were probably the paintings on which Carpaccio modelled his canvas on the same subject. This painting, now in the Serristori Collection in Florence, is a work of extraordinary human compassion. Gentle colour tonalities also denote the *Flight into Egypt* in the National Gallery in Washington, where the figures are set against a silent and enchanted landscape, each one completely isolated in his own emotions.

But there are also other influences noticeable in Carpaccio's work during this period. Gothic and chivalric reminiscences permeate the *Theseus Receiving the Queen of the Amazons* in the Jacquemart André Museum in Paris, a scene taken from the main episode in Boccaccio's *Theseid*; and elements that recall the art of Mantegna, Antonello and the Ferrarese school fill the *Meditation on Christ's Passion* in the Metropolitan Museum in New York, recorded in the 1632 inventory of the Canonici Collection in Ferrara as being by Andrea Mantegna because of a false signature covering Carpaccio's real one. The numerous allusions to the biblical prefigurations of Christ (the figures of Jerome and Job, as well as the inscriptions in Hebrew on the backrests and bases of the thrones) and to the transience of human life (the skull and other bones and the chipped marble)

37

are arranged in a very original way around the truly Bellinian figure of the dead Christ, in slightly archaic style, almost as though these details had been suggested to him by the subject-matter of St Lorenzo Giustiniani's *Sermones*, of Blessed Paolo Giustiniani's *Dialogues on Divine Charity* and Petrarch's *Triumph of Death*.

38   The painting of the *Two Venetian Ladies* in the Correr Museum in Venice probably dates from the beginning of the 16th century; this work was extremely popular in the 19th century, also because of the title that Ruskin gave it, "The Courtesans." In this new, mellow interpretation of colour Carpaccio portrays two ladies relaxing in the cool atmosphere of a garden, surrounded by a marble balustrade. The older one is playing with a couple of dogs, while the other leans languidly on the marble balustrade, holding in her right hand a kerchief, perhaps a token of "bonus amor." In front of her, between the parrot and the peacock that the child shows such an interest in, a pair of ladies' shoes of the kind so popular at the time; the pomegranate on the balustrade next to the

37. *Meditation on Christ's Passion*
70.5 x 87 cm
New York, Metropolitan Museum of Art

38. *Two Venetian Ladies*
94 x 64 cm
Venice, Correr Museum

right-hand dove is a symbolic reference to love and fertility, while the Torella coat-of-arms probably means that the two ladies are members of that Venetian family. In these two women Carpaccio gives us a splendid portrayal of a light and happy mood.

The San Giorgio degli Schiavoni cycle and the first decade of the 16th century

His style enriched thanks to his renewed meditations on the art of Giovanni Bellini, around 1501-2 Carpaccio embarked on his first official commission for the Doges' Palace, a huge canvas to be placed above the Tribunal, the Seat of Judgment, in the Sala dei Pregadi, or Hall of the Senators. We don't know what the subject of the canvas was, but it must have been very important to occupy such a preeminent position; it was destroyed by a fire in 1574, together with other canvases by Giorgione and Titian. The other commission Carpaccio received around this time was a second group of canvases for the headquarters of a minor confraternity, the Scuola degli Schiavoni; this brotherhood was given this name because its members were for the most part Dalmatians, either resident in Venice or sailors and artisans temporarily working there. Built after the Council of Ten passed the legislation governing the institution of confraternities in 1431, on a piece of land belonging to the monasteries of the Hospitalers near the Hospital of Santa Caterina and the church of San Giovanni del Tempio, the building still houses Carpaccio's paintings illustrating episodes from the life of the confraternity's patron saints, Jerome, George and Triphun. In 1551, when the building was restored, the paintings were transferred from the first floor hall to the ground floor. There are also two paintings that 39 are not part of this cycle, the *Agony in the Garden* 40 and the *Calling of Matthew*, dated 1502; and it was in 1502, on 24 April, the feast-day of St George, that during a solemn ceremony Paolo Vallaresso presented to the brotherhood a relic of this saint. Paolo Vallaresso was Venetian Governor in the Peloponnese until he lost the possession to the Turks. In the rather archaic style of the 39 *Agony in the Garden* (a feature which has led several scholars to suggest that it was painted in the last years of the 15th century) we can distinguish certain elements derived from the work of Mantegna, even though they have been modernized thanks to the depth of colour in the evening light, broken only by the flames of the torches carried by the soldiers arriving to the right, outside the walls of Jerusalem. In a completely different vein, the *Calling of Matthew* is much closer to the 40 last episodes of the St Ursula cycle, especially in the precise construction of the colour planes within a composition that is almost exactly similar to that of Giovan Battista Cima's *Miracle of St Mark*, a work painted around 1499 and now in the Staatliche Museen in Berlin. The scene is not set in Capharnaum, but on the Venetian mainland, as we can see from the style of the gate and the buildings around the square, where Matthew, responding to the calling of Jesus Christ and the Apostles, abandons his post as tax-collector (the receipts attached to his worktable indicate that that was indeed his job). Notice the typical wooden parasols placed so as to keep the sunlight off the worktop.

In the seven episodes from the life of the patron saints, taken from Jacobus de Voragine's *Legenda Aurea*, Pietro De Natalibus's *Catalogus Sanctorum* and the *Jeronimus: vita et transitus* published in Venice in 1485, Carpaccio's language is much more mature and self-assured. Following the style of his later canvases from the St Ursula cycle, the artist constructs his compositions with greater freedom and more variety, and he uses full, dense colour values, in perfectly calculated harmonies. The masterpiece is certainly the

39. Agony in the Garden
141 x 107 cm
Venice, Scuola di San Giorgio degli Schiavoni

39

41 *Vision of St Augustine*. The Saint is caught in the instant in which the voice of St Jerome distracts his attention from a letter he was writing to him, to advise him of his imminent death and ascent to heaven. The setting of this miraculous announcement is an idealistic version of the study of a learned Humanist of the period, a cultured man of letters well-versed also in astronomy, sculpture and music. This is clear from the rational organization of the space, the sophisticated furnishings

43 and the variety of the numerous objects displayed on the desk, the bench, the wide platform below, the shelves along the walls, the ledge and the cupboard behind the altar in the niche in the room to the left. Bathed in the strong light that streams in from the windows, every single detail acquires shapes and forms of unparalleled purity: the bindings of the books, the miniatures on the prayerbooks and the pages of the musical texts; the shining gilt studs that hold down the green fabric

42 on the desktop and the red upholstery on the elegant chair and prie-dieu; the little Renaissance sculptures and the gilt bronze statue of the Saviour on the altar; the astrolabes and the large armillary sphere; the little Maltese dog listening to the mysterious voice, intercepting the bright ray of light and projecting, like all the other images, a perfectly sharp and clear shadow. And the extraordinary apparition created by the power of expression of the colour tones, of the shadows, of the vibrant translucent qualities, almost defies description, for this splendid interior is sublimated into a scene of beauty and perfection.

In the other canvases Vittore Carpaccio relies less on his references to the daily life and customs

44 of contemporary Venice. The *St Jerome and the*

46 *Lion* and the *Funeral of St Jerome*, dated 1502, still contain some views that recall the part of the city where the Scuola stood, especially the area around the church of San Giovanni al Tempio and the Hospital of Santa Caterina as they appear in the map of Venice drawn up by Jacopo de' Barbari in 1500. Set in the open square surrounded by carefully planned architectural constructions, the story of St Jerome and the Lion unfolds in several separate episodes, for the most part centering round the figure of the wild beast, tamed by the saint. The monks are shown running in all directions, their blue and white tunics flapping in the wind; the details of the palm trees, the Turks with their turbans and a few exotic animals are the only elements that suggest that the event is actually taking place in Bethlehem, where according to the *Legenda Aurea*, the Bi-

46 shop of Split had retired to. And the *Funeral of St Jerome*, too, takes place in a vaguely Oriental setting, although the buildings in the background, like the ones in the previous canvas, recall the monastery of the Hospitalers in Venice. In fact, here the identification of the Scuola degli Schiavoni is even more plausible: it is the building to the left, in the background, with a sloping roof, round windows and a sort of balcony on the facade. While the previous scene was full of movement, here the atmosphere is quiet, with the monks praying in front of the body of St Jerome and all the empty areas accurately delimited by buildings; only in the centre, on the other side of the walls, can we see a row of hills and a stretch of blue sky. Like all the other events he depicts, Carpaccio also builds the mournful funeral of St Jerome around colour tonalities that transform sentiment and emotion into contemplative calm and serenity.

The power of expression of the colour tonalities is similar also in the *St George and the Dragon*, 47 set in a wide open space, unlike anything Carpaccio had ever done before. The whole of the foreground is taken up by St George on his horse and the monstrous animal, wounded and dying, arranged along a diagonal line that goes from the praying princess to the tip of the dragon's curved tail. On the ground, baked by the sun, where just a few clumps of grass have managed to survive and the trees are dying, we can see the remains of the dragon's victims and vipers, lizards, toads 48 and vultures, each so realistically portrayed that they make this place of death and desolation even more macabre. Only the patches of red of the horse's harness and the princess's dress and the lead grey colour of St George's shining armour break the almost monochrome effect of yellowish browns and pale greens in the foreground and background, separated by the blue of the thin stretch of sea. To the left, from the terraces of the fairytale palaces, the inhabitants of Selene watch the outcome of this extraordinary tournament.

In the preparatory drawing for the *Triumph of* 49,5 *St George*, now in the Uffizi Drawings Collection, the new colour density relies more on the perspective construction and the accurate modelling than is the case in the actual painting, where the lavish costumes of the inhabitants of Selene and 51 the ornate trappings of their horses are arranged like highly colourful stage backdrops on either side of the main event. In the middle, alone, St George deals the dying dragon the final blow. Behind him, the city of Selene stands out against the background of green and brown hills and pale blue sky; despite their Oriental flavour, the buildings are arranged and decorated in a totally Venetian way, especially the large construction in the

40

40. The Calling of Matthew
141 x 115 cm
Venice, Scuola di San Giorgio degli Schiavoni

41

centre, which is somewhat reminiscent of Solomon's Temple or the Kubbet-es Sakbra Mosque in Jerusalem as illustrated in Reeuwich's engravings.

52 The level of expression attained in the first two Schiavoni canvases is not matched by the other two, which were probably painted around 1507, at least according to the date on the scroll on the second step in the *Baptism of the Selenites*. This painting certainly contains details of great richness

53 of colour, such as the group of musicians playing in honour of their King, who is receiving the sacrament of baptism from St George. But there is a definite lack of invention and imagination as we can see from the repetitive architectural background and figure composition. Nor does Carpaccio succeed in minimizing this effect by borrowing elements from paintings by Giovan Battista Cima, such as the *Presentation in the Temple* in the Gemäldegalerie in Dresden. And even more lacking in poetic visual power is the canvas

54,55 showing the *Daughter of Emperor Gordian Exorcized by St Triphun*, where the composition of the scene and the poor use of colour actually suggest the hand of some assistant. In any case, there is no denying that Carpaccio goes through a difficult creative period around the middle of the first decade of the 16th century.

In the first canvases painted for the Scuola di San Giorgio degli Schiavoni Vittore Carpaccio's language, although reaching a poetic highpoint, appeared to be isolated from the rest of the Venetian art scene, which in those early years of the new century was a thriving laboratory of artistic innovation thanks to the presence of Leonardo, Albrecht Dürer and Fra Bartolomeo, as well as the revolutionary colour experiments being carried out by Giorgione, Titian, Sebastiano del Piombo, Lorenzo Lotto and the first suggestions of the new classical art being developed in Florence and Rome by Raphael and Michelangelo. Vittore Carpaccio must have found all but incomprehensible the unrestrainable tension of the modelling in the Rosary that Dürer painted in 1506 for the church of San Bartolomeo, or the independence and powerful originality of colour expression with which the year before Giovanni Bellini in his San Zaccaria Altarpiece modernized his

VICTOR
CARPATHIVS
PINGEBAT

42

43

43. The Vision of St Augustine, detail
Venice, Scuola di San Giorgio degli Schiavoni

44. St Jerome and the Lion
141 x 211 cm
Venice, Scuola di San Giorgio degli Schiavoni

lyrical world, a world that was both human and divine. And he must have been faced with a real dilemma when in 1508, together with Lazzaro Bastiani and Vittore Belliniano, he was asked to assess the value of Giorgione's frescoes in the Fondaco dei Tedeschi: it must have been difficult to express his opinion on that painting full of fresh tonalities, dissolving in degrees of light and mood, a lyrical vision of reality created "without the help of a drawing on paper." An art-form which he saw also in the frescoes painted by Titian or in the extraordinary and impressive organ doors in the church of San Bartolomeo painted in 1508 by another pupil of Giorgione's, Sebastiano del Piombo. Carpaccio must also have understood to what extent his own rational imagination stood in contrast to the intimate and restless interpretation of reality offered by Lorenzo Lotto, an artist who worked in a very different way from Giorgione.

From the last canvases of the Schiavoni cycle we can begin to feel how disconcerted Carpaccio was in the face of these rapid developments taking place in the art scene in Venice; but these signs become much more marked in the Stories from the Life of the Virgin which he painted between 1504 and 1508 in the Scuola degli Albanesi, consecrated to Mary and to St Gall. This building, which still exists, was constructed around the year 1500 on a piece of land belonging to the monastery of the Augustinian friars at San Maurizio; the confraternity it housed consisted mostly of the community of Illyrians who had settled in Venice in great numbers especially after the Turkish conquest of Scutari in 1479. The six small paintings are today in four different museums: the Accademia Carrara in Bergamo (*Birth of the Virgin*), the Brera in Milan (*Presentation in the Temple* and *Wedding of the Virgin*), the Giorgio Franchetti Gallery in the Ca' d'Oro in Venice (*Annunciation* and *Death of the Virgin*) and the Correr Museum in Venice (*Visitation*). The level of invention and innovation in these works is fairly poor, as is the range and depth of colour; this cannot be explained entirely by the fact that Car-

45

45. St Jerome and the Lion, detail
Venice, Scuola di San Giorgio degli Schiavoni

paccio was assisted in this task only by mediocre helpers and that he was less interested in this commission than he had been in the cycle for San Giorgio degli Schiavoni. Carpaccio was quite obviously finding it difficult to develop his art in the climate of spiritual revolution initiated by Giorgione. And yet, in these subjects he occasionally shows a renewed interest in the everyday aspects 56 of existence. Especially in the *Birth of the Virgin* he investigates with great attention to detail the interior scenes, and every last element of the decoration, recreating a mood of intimacy thanks to a use of soft tints, further mellowed by a diffuse lighting.

In the other paintings from this period or immediately later Vittore Carpaccio adds a superior quality of style to his art, keeping his adherence to the rigid canons of perspective construction unaltered and continuing to pay great attention to the definition of his spaces, to the perfect harmony of colours, without basically incorporating any of the novelties being developed around him. In 57 the *Holy Family with Two Donors* in the Gulbenkian Foundation in Lisbon, dated 1505, the broad landscape modelled on the art of Giorgione stands in contrast to the artist's usual practice of not relating the natural atmosphere to the mood of the human figures in the foreground. In a style

which is even more 15th-century, in the *Holy* 58 *Conversation* in the Musée du Petit Palais in Avignon, the figures are lined up on the proscenium, dotting with their bright colours and lights the sun-drenched plateau, behind which, framed by the extraordinary bridge of rock, we find the land- 59 scape background, described in great detail, including hermits going about their daily occupations in natural and architectural settings. These background details were an integral part of the composition from the beginning, as we can see from the preparatory sketch in the Rasini Collection in Milan. This diaphragm between the main figures and the background is reproposed in a simpler relationship in the *Holy Conversations* in the Kunsthalle in Karlsruhe and in the University of Arizona in Tucson, as well as in the *Virgin* 60 *Reading* in the National Gallery in Washington. This last painting is probably a fragment of a much

46. The Funeral of St Jerome
141 x 211 cm
Venice, Scuola di San Giorgio degli Schiavoni

56 larger composition, perhaps a subject developed from the female figure sitting on the balustrade to the right in the *Birth of the Virgin* in the Scuola degli Albanesi. Also dating from this period are both the *Blessing Christ* in the Isaac Delgado
61 Museum of Art in New Orleans and the *Madonna and Blessing Child* in the Washington National Gallery, a painting that is extremely similar to the style of Giovanni Bellini and of Giovan Battista Cima especially in the wide open composition, in the Mother's tender gesture of holding back the Child, in the minutely described landscape with alternating light and shadow even in the furthest corners.

The fact that in his more mature religious works Vittore Carpaccio sees Giovan Battista Cima as a closer and more reliable point of reference, because Cima was another artist who was unwilling to keep constantly up-to-date with the latest inno-

vations in the art language, is noticeable also in altarpieces like the *St Thomas in Glory between St* 62 *Mark and St Louis of Toulouse*, a panel painted in 1507 for the church of San Pietro Martire in Murano and now in the Staatsgalerie in Stuttgart; or like the *Death of the Virgin*, painted in 1508 for the church of Santa Maria in Vado and now in the Pinacoteca in Ferrara, a much more impressive version of the same subject he had painted years before for the Scuola degli Albanesi; and lastly the *Presentation of Christ in the Temple* in the Ac- 63,64 cademia in Venice, painted in 1510, in competition as it were with the grandiose altarpiece that Giovanni Bellini had painted more than twenty years earlier for the same church, San Giobbe. Just as Giovanni Bellini's masterpiece anticipates modern use of colour, to the same extent Carpaccio's is given an enamel-like finish by the light which shapes the sculptural forms set in the perfect architectural composition, a composition of monumental grandeur in a scene which is modelled on the nostalgic and archaic world of Antonello. And yet, keeping these forms of expression unaltered, when the subject matter matches his vocation towards elements of the Humanist culture, Vittore Carpaccio is still capable of producing works of the highest poetry, such as the *Portrait of a Knight*, dated 1510, in the Thys- 65

47

48

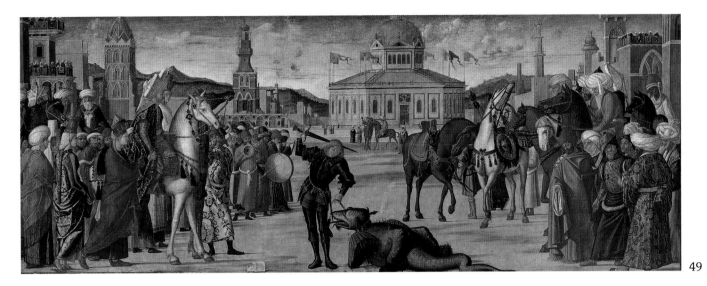

49

47, 48. St George and the Dragon
141 x 360 cm
Venice, Scuola di San Giorgio degli Schiavoni

49. The Triumph of St George
141 x 360 cm
Venice, Scuola di San Giorgio degli Schiavoni

50. The Triumph of St George
Florence, Uffizi Gallery Drawings Collection

sen Collection in Lugano. The young man, standing with his legs slightly apart, is shown as he unsheathes his sword: he dominates the landscape which is also depicted with a Flemish attention to detail. We can distinguish every species of flora and fauna, and with exactly the same accuracy and graphic perfection the profile of the knight on horseback stands out against the walls of the castle; in the foreshortened perspective of the section to the left we can make out a wooden sign of a horse at the gallop. On the opposite side, we can pick out every detail of the city built on the hillside; it is mirrored on the flat surface of the sea and almost blends in the background with the steep rocky mountains. What makes this portrait of the young knight even more fascinating is the

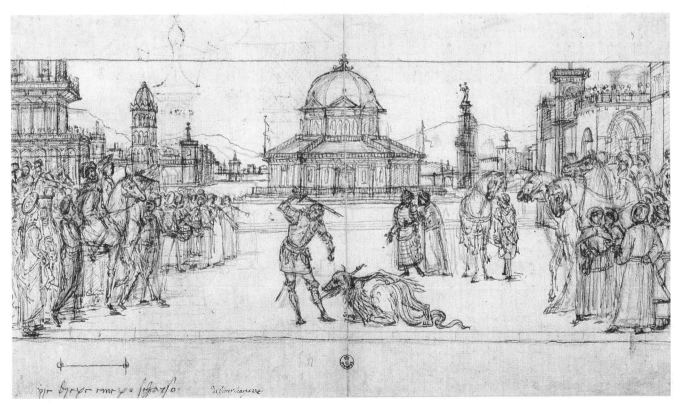

50

51

51. *The Triumph of St George, detail*
Venice, Scuola di San Giorgio degli Schiavoni

52. *The Baptism of the Selenites*
141 x 285 cm
Venice, Scuola di San Giorgio degli Schiavoni

unresolved enigma of his identity; he remains simply the extraordinary, idealized model of many protagonists of the Humanist world, the virtues of which are clearly referred to in the motto "MALO MORI QUAM FOEDARI" (Better to die than to lose one's honour) inscribed on the scroll to the left, above the ermine, a symbol of purity and integrity, while the peacock by the helmet of the armed soldier on horseback is a reference to immortality.

And Vittore Carpaccio must have put the same amount of commitment into the huge canvas of *Pope Alexander III Presenting Doge Sebastiano Zen with the Emblem of the Parasol in Ancona* and also perhaps as Giovanni Bellini's assistant in the other painting, *Pope Alexander III Grants Indulgences to the Faithful Visiting St Mark's on Ascension Day*, two of the paintings commissioned for the Hall of the Supreme Council in the Doges' Palace: the paintings illustrate the role played by Venice in the conflict between Emperor Frederick Barbarossa and Pope Alexander III and were destroyed by the terrible fire of 1577.

The first set of canvases, begun in 1474 by Gentile Bellini, who was later assisted by Alvise Vivarini, was not completed until after 1507 by Giovanni Bellini with the help of Vittore Carpaccio, Vittore Belliniano and another painter called Girolamo. Carpaccio was extremely proud of having been involved in the project, a task that earned him the prestigious title of Official Painter to the Republic. We know this from a letter he wrote to Marquis Francesco Gonzaga on 15 Au-

gust 1511 in which he offers him a "View of Jerusalem" that he praises for "integra paerfectione" and "grandezza." As a guarantee of the quality of the work Carpaccio reminds the Marquis that he is "quello pictor dallo excell. consilio de i diece condutto per dipingere in Salla Granda, dove la Sig.a V.a se dignò a scendere sopra il solaro a veder l'opra nostra che è la historia de Ancona. Et il nome mio è Victor Carpathio" (the painter who was commissioned by the most excellent Council of Ten to paint in the Great Hall, where Your Lordship deigned to come down onto the floor and see our work, a history of Ancona. And my name is Victor Carpathio). From this letter we can see how Carpaccio was worried that his name would be famous only in provincial centres, since the cultural climate of Venice had changed so profoundly both in spiritual values and in visual language. Giorgione died in 1510; in 1511 Sebastiano del Piombo, fascinated by the work of Raphael and Michelangelo, left Venice for Rome; Lorenzo Lotto and Pordenone were constantly travelling throughout Northern and Central Italy; in Venice only the old Giovanni Bellini, until his death in 1516, was capable of renewing his art while still preserving his fully Humanistic mood close to that form of classical use of colour that the young Titian developed even further in his extraordinary career, from the 1511 frescoes in the Scuola del Santo in Padua to the *Assumption* that he painted in 1518 for the central apse in the church of the Frari.

54

53. The Baptism of the
Selenites, detail
Venice, Scuola di San
Giorgio degli Schiavoni

54, 55. The Daughter
of Emperor Gordian is
Exorcized by St Triphun
141 x 300 cm
Venice, Scuola di San
Giorgio degli Schiavoni

55

56

56. *Birth of the Virgin*
126 x 128 cm
Bergamo, Accademia Carrara

57. *Holy Family with Two Donors*
90 x 136 cm
Lisbon, Gulbenkian Foundation

58. *Holy Conversation*
92 x 126 cm
Avignon, Musée du Petit Palais

57

58

59

59. *Holy Conversation, detail*
Avignon, Musée du Petit Palais

60. *The Virgin Reading*
78 x 51 cm
Washington, National Gallery of Art

61. *Madonna and Blessing Child*
85 x 68 cm
Washington, National Gallery of Art

62. *St Thomas in Glory between St Mark and St*
Louis of Toulouse
264 x 171 cm
Stuttgart, Staatsgalerie

63

64

63, 64. *Presentation in the Temple*
421 x 236 cm
Venice, Accademia

65. *Portrait of a Knight*
218 x 152 cm
Lugano, Thyssen Collection

The Stories from the Life of St Stephen and other late works

In the decade during which Titian replaced Giovanni Bellini as the major protagonist of the Renaissance in Venice, Vittore Carpaccio carried out his last important commission. Once again, it was the decoration commissioned by a minor Scuola. The Confraternity of St Stephen, which in 1476 had enlarged its headquarters right near the church consecrated to the saint, on a piece of land belonging to the Augustinians, called on Carpaccio, who was obviously considered the specialist in pictorial cycles of this kind; he was commissioned five canvases illustrating episodes from the life of their patron saint. The canvas of the *Trial of St Stephen* has been lost and the four surviving paintings are now scattered in four 67 different museums. The scene of *St Stephen with Four Followers being Consecrated Deacons by St Peter*, now in the Staatliche Museen in Berlin, is signed and dated 1511; following his typical composition formula, Carpaccio sets the actual event in the foreground, arranged in a series of figure groups articulated in a scansion that creates separate relationships with the landscape, conceived with depth of field and dotted with a great number of complex architectural structures. The use of motifs from his earlier works, primarily from the San Giorgio degli Schiavoni cycle, and the numerous references to the art of Cima, Giovanni Bellini and even Pisanello, detracts from the unity of composition constructed around a colour web woven with deep and full shadowy areas. The two following canvases are actually 68 more successful in this. The *St Stephen Preaching* in the Louvre, which according to Zanetti, who was writing in 1771, bore the date 1514 on the frame, is set on a barren piece of land in front of an ideal view of a city that is reminiscent of Jerusalem. The buildings of this imaginary city form a spacious arc in the lower section and then climb up the ridge of the hill, following the zigzagging path that leads to the place where St Stephen, standing atop a classical pillar, is addressing a group of Oriental characters. Their costumes and headdresses create a splendidly varied play of colours that stands out against the pale green field. In the scene of the *Disputation of* 69 *St Stephen* in the Brera Pinacoteca, the saint is shown below a wide and spacious loggia, clearly modelled on the architecture of Pietro Lombardo, placed slightly at an angle. On the bases of the columns in the foreground, in the most visible place, Vittore Carpaccio signed his name and inscribed the date, 1514. Around the deep greens and browns of the Venetian hills he has arranged a series of buildings, in a varied combination of architectural styles which suggest a fairytale Orient and a Western world that is also a product of the imagination. In this painting Carpaccio gives his imagination free rein, creating the most eccentric architectural constructions of any of his works; such as the equestrian monument placed on very high marble supports pierced by free-standing sculptures; or the pyramid that blends into the 70 opalescent sphere; or the elaborate building to the right, next to the walls that recede in a typical diagonal perspective foreshortening. Against this totally imaginary architectural background, highlighted and animated by the colour patches of the groups of characters, Carpaccio has given us a series of concrete and realistic portraits, probably of members of the confraternity who were much more interested in having their portrait painted than they were in the debate between St Stephen and the Orientals. The last canvas of the cycle, painted many years later as we can see from the date, 1520, on the scroll, shows the *Stoning of St* 71 *Stephen*; it is now in the Staatsgalerie in Stuttgart. Here Carpaccio displays a totally mannered use of colour, bright and translucid in the scene of the martyrdom, and soft and veiled in the depiction of the mythical Jerusalem, enclosed by its high walls, each detail of its buildings described with

66

care, and in the groups of figures themselves, patches of colour that shine in the light that varies according to the filtering action of the clouds in front of the sun.

The quality of Carpaccio's use of colour and his power of expression and invention decrease even further in his last religious paintings, for the most part executed by his assistants: the Polyptych of Santa Fosca, 1514, now dismembered (Correr Museum in Venice, National Gallery in Zagreb, Accademia Carrara in Bergamo), and the altarpiece of the church of San Vitale in Venice dating

72 from the same year; the *Crucifixion of the Ten Thousand Martyrs on Mount Ararat* (1515) in the Accademia and the autograph portrayal of the proud *St Paul* (1520) in the church of San Domenico in Chioggia; the polyptychs and altarpieces he painted for several small centres in the Republic's dominions, such as Pozzale (1519), Capodistria (1516-1523), Pirano (1518). But in at least two of his late works, where the subject matter stimulated his imagination, Carpaccio returned to the creative levels of his earlier peri-

73 ods. The *Lion of St Mark*, painted in 1516 for the Magistrato dei Camerlenghi in Rialto and today in the Doges' Palace, is an imposing creation, standing with its hind legs in the water and its forelegs on dry land, one firmly resting on a rocky shore and the other holding up the book with the tradi-

66, 67. St Stephen is Consecrated Deacon
148 x 231 cm
Berlin-Dahlem, Gemäldegalerie

68

tional inscription PAX/TIBI/MAR/CE/E/VANGE-LI/STA/MEUS. This image symbolizing the power on land and sea of the Venetian Republic is particularly significant if we consider that it was painted just after the Serenissima had run the risk of losing its independence when it was attacked by the League of Cambrai, the coalition of great powers formed in 1509. Behind the symbol of St Mark, portrayed in splendid and triumphant isolation, Carpaccio has given us a view of some of the places where the fortunes of the Serenissima had prospered and grown for more than five centuries. In this extraordinary wide-angled view the artist gives us a perfectly detailed depiction of the basin of St Mark's towards San Nicolò di Lido, all the way to the heart of Venice: the Doges' Palace, St Mark's Basilica, the columns of St Theodore and St Mark, the Piazzetta, the bell-tower and the Clock Tower.

A totally different mood prevails in the *Dead Christ* now in the Staatliche Museen in Berlin, which in fullness and richness of colour resembles the 1520 *Stoning of St Stephen*; it is a later ver-

68. St Stephen Preaching
152 x 195 cm
Paris, Louvre

69. The Disputation of St Stephen
147 x 172 cm
Milan, Pinacoteca di Brera

sion of the *Meditation on Christ's Passion* in the 37
Metropolitan Museum in New York, and like it it
was mentioned in 1623 in the Collection of
Roberto Canonici in Ferrara as being by Andrea
Mantegna. With the light accentuating the waxy
pallor of his flesh, Christ is rigidly stretched out on
the shiny marble slab, as though suspended in the
foreground of the painting. Against the background of the rocky earth a number of symbols of
death all relate to Christ's life on earth and suggest
the transience of human life: we see the Virgin,
supported by Mary Magdalene in front of St
John, a mourning figure with his back to the spectator; St Job in meditation leaning against a tree;
graves opened and violated, broken and shat-
tered tombstones, columns and slabs.

We know that Carpaccio received further com-
missions from Patriarch Antonio Contarini in
1522 and 1523 and that he was still alive on 28
October 1525, as we learn from a document

70. The Disputation of St Stephen, detail
Milan, Pinacoteca di Brera

71. The Stoning of St Stephen
142 x 170 cm
Stuttgart, Staatsgalerie

signed by his wife in 1527. He died sometime before 26 June 1526, as we are told in a testimony given by his son Pietro. Although in the last period of his career his art was undeniably conventional and unimaginative, for the most part Carpaccio's work displayed extraordinary originality within the Venetian artistic tradition, with solid roots in the civilization of the late Quattrocento. Already in the early 1490s his artistic language reached its full power of expression, the result of various influences and models attained from all the most learned spheres of Humanism. As though through a perfect photographic diaphragm, forms, colours, lights and shadows are reproduced without any hierarchical privileges, with exceptional clarity, not bound by any kind of atmospherical relationship, within carefully calculated and accurate compositional organizations. This kind of presentation of a world devoid of

72

72. *The Crucifixion of the Ten Thousand Martyrs on Mount Ararat*
307 x 205 cm
Venice, Accademia

74

73. The Lion of St Mark
130 x 368 cm
Venice, Doges' Palace

74. The Lion of St Mark,
detail of the basin of St Mark's looking towards San Nicolò di Lido
Venice, Doges' Palace

75. The Lion of St Mark,
detail of the Doges' Palace and St Mark's Basilica
Venice, Doges' Palace

76. The Dead Christ
145 x 185 cm
Berlin-Dahlem, Gemäldegalerie

77. The Dead Christ, detail
Berlin-Dahlem, Gemäldegalerie

mystery and anguish continued even during the radical spiritual revolution that took place in the first two decades of the 16th century in Venice. Basically, Carpaccio remained untouched by this rapid change of artistic style: he did not take part in it, he merely witnessed it. Actually, it even seems as though he wanted to contrast it, to oppose it, with his own means of expression, to compete with these totally innovative and revolutionary developments: that his only interest was in transposing objective reality into enchanted dreams of a purely symbolic value, with no idealistic intentions at all and no inclination towards "modern" realism. It must indeed have been his choice to follow this proud but difficult path that explains why he had neither an organized workshop nor any talented followers. And it probably explains why Carpaccio has always been relegated by art historians to the role of a genre painter, a painter of superficial narratives, at least until modern scholars first recognized his unique creative talents.

Short bibliography

G. VASARI, *Le vite dei più eccellenti architetti, pittori et scultori italiani*, Florence, 1550 and 1568 (Ed. Milanesi, III, Florence, 1868).

C. RIDOLFI, *Le maraviglie dell'arte*, Venice, 1648 (Ed. Hadeln, Berlin, 1914).

M. BOSCHINI, *Le ricche miniere...*, Venice, 1674.

A. M. ZANETTI, *Della pittura veneziana...*, Venice, 1771.

J. RUSKIN, *St. Mark's Rest*, Kent, 1877.

B. BERENSON, *The Venetian Painters of the Renaissance*, New York-London, 1894, 1907, 1911.

C. LUDWIG, P. MOLMENTI, *Vittore Carpaccio. La vita e le opere*, Milan, 1906.

A. VENTURI, *Storia dell'arte italiana*, vol. VII, part IV, Milan, 1915.

R. VAN MARLE, *The Development of the Italian Schools*, The Hague, 1936.

B. BERENSON, *Italian Pictures of the Renaissance - Venetian School*, London, 1957.

C. L. RAGGHIANTI, *Vittore Carpaccio*, in "Selearte", X, 1962.

R. LONGHI, *Viatico per cinque secoli di pittura veneziana*, Florence, 1946.

V. MOSCHINI, *Carpaccio. La leggenda di Sant'Orsola*, Milan, 1948.

T. PIGNATTI, *Carpaccio*, Milan, 1955.

B. BERENSON, *Pittura italiana del Rinascimento. La Scuola Veneta*, vol. I, Florence, 1958.

G. FIOCCO, *Carpaccio*, Novara, 1958.

R. PALLUCCHINI, *I teleri del Carpaccio in San Giorgio degli Schiavoni*, Milan, 1961.

J. LAUTS, *Carpaccio*, London, 1962.

M. MURARO, *Carpaccio*, Florence, 1966.

P. ZAMPETTI, *Vittore Carpaccio*, Venice, 1966.

G. PEROCCO, *L'opera completa di Vittore Carpaccio*, Milan, 1967.

M. MURARO, *I disegni di Vittore Carpaccio*, Florence, 1977.

V. SGARBI, *Carpaccio*, Bologna, 1979.

F. VALCANOVER, *Le storie di Sant'Orsola di Vittore Carpaccio dopo il recente restauro*, in "Atti dell'Istituto Veneto di Scienze, Lettere e Arti", Venice, CXLIV, 1985/86.

L. ZORZI, *Carpaccio e la rappresentazione di Sant'Orsola*, Turin, 1988.

77

Index of illustrations

Other Authors: